Lessons in Space

University of Central Florida
Contemporary Poetry Series

University Press of Florida

GAINESVILLE TALLAHASSEE TAMPA BOCA RATON

PENSACOLA ORLANDO MIAMI JACKSONVILLE

Lessons in Space

CATHLEEN CALBERT

Copyright 1997 by the Board of Regents of the State of Florida
Printed in the United States of America on acid-free paper
All rights reserved

02 01 00 99 98 97   C   6 5 4 3 2 1

02 01 00 99 98 97   P   6 5 4 3 2 1

Library of Congress Cataloging-in-Publication Data
Calbert, Cathleen.
Lessons in space / Cathleen Calbert.
p. cm. — (Contemporary poetry series)
ISBN 0–8130–1502–2 (cloth: alk. paper). —
ISBN 0–8130–1503–0 (pbk.: alk. paper)
I. Title. II. Series: Contemporary poetry series (Orlando. Fla.)
PS3553.A39448L47 1997
811'.54—DC21   96-49005

The University Press of Florida is the scholarly publishing agency for
the State University System of Florida, comprised of Florida A & M
University, Florida Atlantic University, Florida International Univer-
sity, Florida State University, University of Central Florida, University
of Florida, University of North Florida, University of South Florida,
and University of West Florida.

University Press of Florida
15 Northwest 15th Street
Gainesville, FL 32611

for my mother

Contents

Acknowledgments

Grateful acknowledgment is made to the publications in which the following poems first appeared, sometimes in different versions:

13th Moon: "Girlfriends"
The Anthology of New England Writers: "A Blue Cup, with a Crack"
Bogg: "All That Is Known To Be Beautiful"
Callapooya Collage: "Panda Problems"
The Hudson Review: "Silent Men"
The Nation: "Fainting," "School-yard"
Nimrod: "Dad," "Garden Grove," "Mysterious Weather," "Lessons in Space," "A Small Cross" (under the title "Losing his Mother")
The North American Review: "Babysitting"
The Ohio Review: "Playhouse"
Ploughshares: "Living with Monkeys"
Poetry Northwest: "A Train Is Going to Germany"
Shenandoah: "Cajun Wings and Loaded Skins"
Western Humanities Review: "Blackberry"

"Fainting" was reprinted in the anthology *Catholic Girls.*
"Young Man at the Family Planning Clinic" was corecipient of the Gordon Barber Memorial Award from the Poetry Society of America in 1994.

I am grateful to the MacDowell Colony, Rhode Island College, the Rhode Island Council for the Arts, and Yaddo for their generous support.

Special thanks to Philip Booth, Katryn Hansen, Richard Howard, David Lazar, Barbara Mortimer, and especially my husband and helpmate, Christopher Mayo.

Garden Grove

I didn't see the waves of orange trees
turn to dust though I did witness
the emergence of The Malabar,

Dana Andrews' sudden complex
of white squares where fair divorcées
could live close to their mistakes.

Those apartments were strangely placed
in the dead land of railroad tracks,
ruining what had been weed-softened dens

for poor lovers and taking away
the summer ease of a suburban swamp
full of pollywogs for young fishermen.

Perhaps it was the disappearing
stories of orange groves disappearing
that first shook my faith in things.

Or not. After all, I was just a girl,
barefoot all summer and lazy, unless
gutter-walking in my Zoris, filthy,

my one skill reciting the *TV Guide*'s
schedule of prime-time programming.
Life was easy. Sure, there was fighting:

my father lifting the kitchen table in the air,
blood and mustard skidding down my legs
as we ran, my mom and us kids,

to the deserted school-yard, where I
forswore him, my father still calling
for his gun, his wife. I vowed to fight;

instead, I left. I had things but lost them
as I moved in six-month fits of longing.
I loved someone, but I went away.

Still, born to the floating homes of those
who were hurt all the way to the edge
of the country, I carry with me:

my fainting away before the priest,
salt water washing my body,
the desire to slip away unseen.

A shakiness in thought, maybe.
One badly formed, lopsided smile.
Unbelievable memories of innocence.

Fainting

Those steps, cooler than I could have believed,
and my face in absolute harmony.
At last, the collapse of my body.
Only my cheeks, toes, fingers remaining.
Then the voices of men or, more often, women
in tones of despairing angels, devoted solely to me,
calling from above. Each moment, a miracle,
and I suddenly wonderful, a child Hermione:
"Look! Her eye's opening. The color's returning."
When my flesh awoke, drops of water blessed
the top of my head to the soles of my feet.
From other children, it's true, there was
some mean-spirited talk of ray-guns
and susceptibility. Well, we were all
trapped in church, and it wasn't their fault
if they couldn't stop breathing.
Not for them, the drama, being lifted by
strange men and whisked away. Yes, the beauty
of it was not being guilty of anything, for I tried
to hold on, my uneven curls unraveling, and I
watching my hands press together, the white gloves,
a little wicker purse dangling from one wrist.
Inside: a hanky and a dime. I tried waiting
until I could walk down the aisle and be given
a little something to suck on, always comforting,
the wafer dissolving on the roof of my mouth,

like Chinese paper candy, mysterious and lingering.
Then I'd be happy, and it would be ending.
But sometimes I'd need to leave early,
and a child doesn't leave easily.
I'd wait until it was too late,
until my eyes were large and dark as I
tried to find my mother's face. "Why
didn't you tell me?" Then the rush
to lay me out, in the air, on the concrete,
ladies pulling down my dress, trying to press
my knees together (they would not stop dividing),
waking to promises from my repentant mother
of love and new Sunday mornings until everyone
gave up on my legs and talked softly to me.
So Emily was wrong to be afraid, wasn't she?
For I knew then, I knew I could be controlled
only until I let go.

The Blessed Virgin

I waited until all the lights were off,
after the others had foolishly fought

over who would sleep with Kitty—my father
swearing we should keep her outside—and I

crept, guilty as a lover, small as a child,
full of innocence and my dirty tricks,

none too clean, being bathed once a week,
to my mother's side, where I finger-curled

her curly hair, forming tree after red tree,
following her pattern of breathing with my own

where she had gone, into dreams, and the queen-
sized mattress—for my mother, Mary, Queen

of Heaven, Mother of God—went spinning off
into space, cool, high, silent, far away,

circling in the center of pure, white stars
as I tried my best not to fall to my death,

making myself as heavy as a child can be
to stay forever in her weightless bed.

All That Is Known To Be Beautiful

I never got animals right: legs of graceless horses
splayed four ways, none hitting the line of ground
I'd carefully scrawled across the page, though I made
each eye hugely pretty and able to gaze independently.

Their ears, intended small, grew by degrees to rabbit-size,
suddenly full and fine, like feathers stuck wondrously
atop their heads. Each animal became a new species,
so ill-formed as to be near extinction when complete.

I kept creating lamb-dogs, camel-cows, human-does.
And was always disillusioned. When at last I grew too old
to give long lashes or lovely lips to these beasts, someone
helped put them to sleep: "Good use of color; no sense of line."

I've tried to leave them alone since then, yet sometimes
my hand moves on its own, and horses leak free, crippling
their hooves on awkwardly drawn streets, still denying
all that is known to be beautiful by so strangely dancing.

Junior High

Neon shoes,
         usually blue.
A
      padded
                blue
                     bra
                          (contoured, I
assured myself)
      plus
the essential Juicy Fruit.
                          In diary,
my white lips
breathed, "Jay
                is
                     so
                          cool,"
for simply,
         virgin-stilled,
it was true.

Babysitting

They are girls, making a little money,
having some fun, trying on Red Devil
lip gloss, painting the moons of their nails
since the babies are in bed. But there's a call
from a man who says he can see them,
right next door, with two children
tied up beside him. They're scared,
he says, and it seems that one is
beginning to bleed. They need to listen
to him carefully: he wants the girls
to do some tricks or he'll kill the kids
so they better be quick about it.
Both friends hold their breaths,
bright mouths in little o's. He says,
"Take off your clothes. Go to the window.
Touch each other for me." The red fades
to pink as they kiss, feeling nothing.
They are moving farther from their bodies;
only their bowels retain sensation:
turning cold. Everything else is gone.
The room blackens, the man's voice softens,
fading to a dream, but he's holding on,
telling them to do new things
with their bodies, open up everything
at fourteen. He doesn't know the girls
have floated far above his pleas

until one says, "We're through.
We have nothing to do with you."
They lie apart on the carpet then,
both of them gently shivering
into their skins, their pink fingers
interlaced as they wait for sirens,
knowing innocents may be dying,
but no man is found, no children;
no one is even living in that house.

Dad

Fat, in boxer shorts and undershirt, he leaned back
his easy-chair, telling stories of spending the war
in a submarine, and I listened, thinking of sardines,
men packed in each other's sweat deep within the sea.

Photos of Hawaiian cuties on R&R. Tales of native men
rushing into shallow water, how he thought they kissed
the fish until being told they sucked out the eyes:
a delicacy. Everything he said became scary.

His bedtime story, the dead woman's revenge again:
"Johnny, I'm on the ninth step, Johnny, I'm on the tenth step.
Johnny! I've got you!" God, his dark eyes, way with words,
my pleasure-screams full of fear for the murderer.

At his casket, the priest could only think to say, "Mickey
liked a good joke." The ape mask at midnight. Frog legs
popping with salt as they fried. And salt too for the trick
with the fly he'd dunk, then bless, crying, "Lazarus, arise!"

Letting the crabs loose in the living room, telling me,
"They'll sink their claws in so deep you'll never get free."
Plopping me on the fridge, laughing, threatening to leave.
A mad chase with raw beef tongue clenched in his teeth.

There were all those animals too: Pancho, the blue
parrot, tucked under his shirt as we crossed the border,
roosters named for parish priests, an alligator who lived
in our bathtub for three weeks before giving up the ghost.

Monkeys flown in from Florida nestled against his oily hair,
curling their fingers around his ear with a kind of love
or tearing worms in two, sucking the halves like Popsicles.
He trained them to attack if we came too near his chair:

a joke, a game. Though never to me. I tried to recede
into the background of the family, playing mermaids
in the ivy, ignoring snails and broken glass, digging deeply
into the spade-shaped leaves, moving toward invisibility.

"You son of a bitch, you farmer, you woman!" I remember
all the slurs he yelled at others while swerving crazily.
When I said, "Slow down, you're scaring me," he told me,
"That's what these schmucks expect when they see a Grand Prix."

Maybe he was in a rage from days spent on the L.A. freeway,
dressing all those display windows along the way, arranging
dummies into good-looking scenes. All I know is at night
I prayed, "God, don't let him come home again."

But we were the ones who left: his wife, his children, one dying
monkey whose tail was rotting away, our German Shepherd
dragging his back legs, the rabbit waiting to escape, my own dog
who would die in the new streets of a poorer neighborhood.

Even the tortoises, who never did anything but swallow dandelions,
found a way of disappearing. All else had been placed in the soil
of home, near the daffodils or palm tree, our yard the scene of a hundred
funerals, toothpick crosses long since faded into the same earth.

He last saw me when I was sixteen. He said he knew I would move
to Oakland and go with black men. He didn't live to see me live
in New York with a Jew. If he were here, I could condemn him. Or forgive.
In dreams, we're always talking, but I never hear what he's saying.

Living with Monkeys

It's not a nice thing.
Not a nice idea. Or it might be
a nice idea. Who knows?
King Kong. Mighty Joe Young. Cheetah.
But it's not nice, not really.
Living with monkeys is not pretty.
Beside the quart of chocolate milk
(which had to be divided equally,
my brothers and sister slowly measuring),
live worms in plastic containers
were kept bean-dip-style in the refrigerator
because a monkey likes to eat such things,
and it pleased my father to please a monkey.
They were all his idea, after the guinea pigs
had eaten their offspring, and we had
lost the parrot, abandoned the alligator.
Sometimes they can die pretty quickly.
One did of TB, all animal ethereal,
looking like Mother Theresa, like Gandhi,
swaddled in white towels, and rocked
to its end by my mother who hated it
and who wouldn't stop weeping
over this, her last and strangest baby.
The other thrived on special treats.
Sometimes my brothers gave it something
dazzling to eat (a cricket or a lizard)

and watched happily as the littlest hands
in the family ripped up little living things.
Oh, they had little hands, little nails,
eyelids, eyelashes, and their eyes
beyond reason, human, inhuman.
Do you know what it's like
to look a monkey eye to eye?
A real monkey who likes to bite,
who will challenge you to fight
for your food or your right to pass by?
Why would anyone think this was good?
How long could this life be withstood?
When my father parted ways with the family,
we knew what to do: leave that monkey outside!
He stayed in his cage, cold and unclean,
while we went on our desperate first dates,
coming home to smoke dope as we sat in the swings
of the rusty swing-set left by a younger family
in the rented backyard full of yellow thistles
and anonymous, vicious, little dogs
who liked to fly up and bite
down our clothes from the clothesline.
And when the last monkey finally died,
and the dogs had run away,
and our cat had run away,
we knew what to do: we changed
jobs, changed schools, left friends,
and moved closer to the ocean,
so we could start all over again.

School-yard

Nothing's as hushed as a school-yard
holding only one girl, her dog, and two boys
who hide as she swings high as she can,
hard as she can push away from the soft
ground on a gray day, a Sunday,

while a mother begins Lemon Chicken,
as a father eases his clean car into place,
while a sister rolls her hair over cans,
as brothers smoke reefer and listen
wistfully to Puff the Magic Dragon.

Silent, this girl in her favorite sweater,
the red one. A child who rarely speaks.
Is there something wrong with her?
Some say she's too close to her mother.
And she's afraid of her father.

She's the baby of the family. So why
is she alone in the school-yard? But why
shouldn't she be alone? Isn't she always?
For girls are alone in their silence,
wrapped in the silence of their cocoons,

twirling in the front yard, fantasizing,
or hidden behind their mothers, sipping
sugary coffee, listening to who's done what
to whom, discovering: Mrs. Bradford's not
so happy. Mrs. Bradford's husband's boring.

What happens more slowly and secretly
than two boys stopping a girl as she moves
in her cocoon, in her red sweater, her dog
beside her? Their words are whispers, too close,
and too far away, a new system of symbols,

the world swerving to a new kind of time
with minutes made of pulses as one boy
opens his shirt and pulls out a long knife.
He asks, has she ever seen this long a knife.
She answers, yes, she's seen her father's swords.

With the raising of blades,
the boys know they can say anything,
so one of them threatens to run her dog
through, the other whispers, "I love you,"
as he unbuttons her pants to touch her inside.

And they become a tableau:
the small dog watching anxiously, a thin boy
with his head turned away—a look-out or ashamed?
The other pressing the girl into a wall as she gazes
beyond this unfolding scene, years of silence,

of silently playing, helping her not to see
what is happening, until the spell breaks,
the boys run, and she too runs, her dog in her arms.
She is a heroine, after all: she's saved her Junior's life.
She tells him so, speaking, it seems endlessly,

until coming home, where her mother pours her water
and wants to know: did he bounce up and down on her.
That's what she asks: "Did he bounce up and down?"
Her brothers rush out, ready to fight any number
of knives, her sister cries about bad reputations,

and her father asks a single question: "Why
didn't you scream?" For years, she'll repeat,
"Why didn't you scream?" Though no one will speak
again of silence, of a girl in a red sweater, alone
in the school-yard, on a gray day, a Sunday.

Silent Men

Who were they? That generation, those men. Such mysteries.
I believe that men were bigger then, their backsides wide,
their faces manly and mean, or sunken in within their own miseries.
But all I have are fragments, details, sensory memories

of my father, who smelled of Wild Turkey, Old Spice, Brylcreem,
and something like a man's leather jacket worn in the rain
or the chamois he used to smooth over the curves of his cars.
What drove him? How can I decipher his devotions?

I know only the periphery. He enjoyed deep-sea fishing,
coming home loaded down with the huge, bloody things
that he clomped in the house and dumped in the sink,
filling all of us with the smell of blood and fish and the sea.

It's true it was good, the fresh catch he folded in foil,
baked in mayonnaise and lemons, the best I've ever eaten.
I believed in that flesh I tasted some of where he'd been.
But I couldn't be certain. He didn't take us with him.

Who knew what men did on their own? Not my mother,
who stayed at home. Nothing was told. He had his own room
with a lock, and he had a key he carried with him into the world
when he'd leave, sealing up the king-sized bed where he made us

stay if we were bad on Saturdays, stolen fairy-tale children
who'd awoken the ogre from his drunken sleeping. Struck dumb,
I watched the wallpaper, a lady's choice, all lilacs and tea roses,
stained yellow with his hair oil, and I wondered at his clutter

of male things: the *Playboys* I would be punished for touching,
glass rings on the night-stand, glass ashtrays left heaping,
matches from The Red Lantern, The Spanish Gypsy, the ham radio
so he could play submarine, this sailor lost at sea, submerged

in a fatherhood born of unexpected pregnancies and believing
he could somehow do the right thing, stranded though he was
in the suburbs of southern California, too far away from
the silent lakes of Michigan and a large, immigrant family.

He'd run off at sixteen. At twenty, he rode his Hog across
the country. In his fifties, he planted daffodils and served me
tiny highballs in glasses with naked ladies and racy sayings.
It's true a few times I too attempted to befriend him,

coquettishly plucking the Rice Krispie moles on his shoulder,
trying my tongue on "Daddy," wondering what life would be like
as a real daughter with a real father I could say things to
without that awful falsehood ringing through, for, truly,

I hated how he teased me, and I was already beyond his reach.
I froze in poses, falling in place in my own game of Statues.
I was Helen Keller. I was Through the Looking Glass.
As for him, I thought he must belong to the Mob.

After all, he was always standing at the edge of things,
distant, shadowed, smoking, some underworld figure
who could ice his enemies, whose own family hated him
coming home dead drunk, dark-eyed, angry, so

when he did bang in, we all slunk off to our rooms, though
a few times he put a halt to this retreat, seeming to think
he needed to teach us something, and he told my brothers,
who feared him, not to knock a girl up, and they never did,

and he told my sister, who loved him, she looked like a slut,
so she did, and he told me, though I wanted nothing to do
with him, I couldn't be trusted: I'd already been molested.
He tried to run over the boys after they'd been arrested.

At least, he trashed their mailboxes with his Grand Prix,
and it was their turn to call the police. What possessed him?
Was it love of me? It must have hurt to see me spring
past his hands, always running to my mother, who was

concentrating her energy on hating him until she finally dyed
her hair red and got a job that let her be in a uniform and sleep
with a fireman, and we saw our father on obligatory visits
to his new bachelor pad, where he passed his evenings

making stupid things: mosaic ashtrays, tiny blue tiles
neatly arranged, or jokes, like his plaque to display
"The Family Jewels" (two walnut halves glued in place),
which he hung next to his old navy cartoons:

"Broad on Starboard Bow" and "Saluting the Waves."
I believe I missed the meaning of these and many things.
Even now, I can just pen a silhouette of him, the dark
image of my girlhood dreams, which I can show all

my friends when we share our stories of the same
drinking, silence, rage, that have left us wondering,
Who were they? Those men, that generation, the fathers
of such accomplished and such fucked-up daughters.

Sluts

For Suzie, Lucy, Lynda, and Terry

What "slut" means is hard and easy,
as in tough don't-fuck-with-me cookie and freely shooting
    the breeze
in high-school bathrooms, ratting that nasty hair, getting high,
chiding the other girls who file silently through to wash
    their hands
before they hurry back to the goodness of teachers and boys in
    clean sweaters
and can shake off the gibes of the bad girls left applying deep
    purple shadow to their eyes,
the sluts talking trash about their own tits and about cock size
until graduating to the dark bars, where they are willing to hang
    until forever ends,
though they are never really easy, never softly resting in the arms
    of somebody,
even caressed as they may be, temporarily at least, by someone, a
    new lover
who hasn't slapped a tooth loose or run up their credit cards,
they're braced, they're ready, their elbows sharp, at right angles,
their painted nails hard and dark and long as claws
or bitten into the skin of their fingers as though they long to
    gnaw off their own limbs,
waiting for the blow, for the trouble that's always coming,

the trouble that seems to follow wherever the hell they go,
so they stay wary, watchful, on guard, always off-center
 and edgy,
never seeming able to stand up straight or stay upright
 and steady,
slouched over in a way a lady never would, twisted, languid,
their tight or fat, sassy, sullen asses stuck up in the air,
their posture contrapuntal, their attitude punk,
showing off that terrible something that's just too loose
 in them,
even when their bodies are razor-thin, little-girl skinny,
their hair unkempt, greased and teased high, or lank, uncut,
 hanging over one eye
with its heavy liner pointing out the end, slanted like a cat's,
their lips bruised or illuminated with dollar lipstick that
 smells like penny candy,
like a good time at a side-walk fair that will be torn down in
 the morning,
their leather purses old and oily, smelling like wild animals,
legs gray in off-black stockings, a run high on the thigh or a
 little nick at the knee
from kneeling God knows where doing God knows what,
silver anklets engraved with their names, and mean-looking
 shoes, thin, high, pointed unnaturally,
or even kick-ass boots, and underneath, the black underwire
 and black panties,
or nothing at all, just their too-tight clothes, slick and fragrant
against their pale and sallow skins, their cheeks lightly scarred,
eerie under the heavy pancake, even slightly green, as if they
have had to drag their sorry asses out of bed every morning of
 their lives,
dig into burned black coffee, cop-heavy, coffee-shop jelly
 donuts, greasy chips, and start smoking again,
as though they never have taken in much of anything that's
 good for them,
never would be seen, for example, munching an apple with
 strong, white, horse teeth
(never even be imagined jogging in white shorts down
 a sunlit beach); indeed,

their teeth are bad, crooked, discolored, uneven, sexy little
	evil things,
laced with silver fillings that gleam when they lean back
	to laugh,
and when they lean forward again, smirking, you can see one
	front tooth
bent lazily over the other, as though they are in bed together,
	like the sluts
themselves who are scorned by nice girls and even by the men
	who see them,
as they roar around town in their loud cars with their
	v-8 engines,
their thin black skirts and the jeans that are creased into
	the cracks
of their hard and easy bodies, their jackets short, red, leather,
	or dyed
rabbit skins slowly unfolding, pelt by pelt, from someone's
	poor job of sewing,
and their visible hickeys, the dark marks of long nights,
	all ending
in the spilling of salty fluid from their bodies
as they call out, "Hey, wait a minute, don't leave me,"
jangling the necklaces that leave bands of brassy green around
	their breakable necks,
and their menthol cigarettes and their 2 A.M. faces,
and their lousy hygiene, and their lousy taste in friends,
and their foul mouths, full of gutter talk and challenges,
and their feminine tattoos, the signs they carry on their bodies
of who they've been, of what they are:
a rose, a dove, a cross, a star.

The Land of Milk and Honey

Many things made you happy: Disneyland fireworks
viewed from your roof, sewer mud, sprinkler-jumping,
but most of all the movies: a thrill being somewhere else,
swilling tap water from old soda bottles, plunging
your hands into bags of home-made popcorn.

Then the pleasures of promiscuity, adolescence
in southern California, that land of similes.
It was like, really easy where you were free
to voice a perpetual need for reassurance,
you know, you know what I mean.

Well, beaten-down beach towns
rarely seem to mean much of anything.
Just the rocking of the waves, that rhythm,
fondling a boy on a blue Mexican horse blanket,
over the damp sand, below the stars.

What luck: sweetly drunk on sloe gin,
Southern Comfort. Eating tacos,
wiping the grease on your unzipped jeans,
your neck soaked in moon and blue bruises,
your smokes Kool, your breath Wintergreen.

Then you learn about heritage in New York City,
how it's good to have and how you don't have any.
A void: your oasis of sweet date shakes, sloppily

drunk at the best fruit shack you found along
the soft shoulder of the Pacific Coast Highway,

a wasteland of sensuous landscape, nothing
but sex on the beach, hanging at Bob's or Denny's,
manners unbecoming. Your cheeks turn pink
when your New Yorker presses your hands
closer to the plate as you cut up a steak.

He wants to know if you know what "antipasto"
means, so you slowly stop serving rum and Coke
in the morning, knock off Kahlua as an aperitif,
though the mysteries of shellfish and chopsticks
are safe, and silverware's a perpetual uncertainty.

Then when you head west again, your easy
slang refined to stuttering, someone's ruby ring
at odds with the big, pink hands that serve
to identify a waitress who once dished it out
at a greasy spoon, boardwalk dive, you find yourself

hating your family, even your favorite brother,
that handsome apple of your eye, slicked up
and polished for the city, when he slips out
a bottle of peach brandy at the movies,
laughs too loudly, and passes it on to you.

Playhouse

We were our own Mama and Papa.
We had our own little house,
and we were in hiding, like
Anne Frank, so it was exciting.

I liked when you circled me in
your arms, telling me you loved me,
though I trembled to hear you say
how you'd bash out his brains

with the bat between your legs
if our father discovered us
where our mother had hidden us
in the pink-shuttered playhouse

he had made for us and used once
as the backdrop for picture-taking,
having posed us as grown-ups,
as our own little family:

Cheryl, a lovely señorita.
You, stiff and serious in a bow tie,
reading the paper, smoking a pipe.
A baby, I played the baby.

II.

When I could run after you,
you let me be nurse to your dying
soldier as you fell in the sweet dirt
of the peach and apricot trees,

cut down in your youth, stopped
dead in your tracks, stabbed
in the eyes, shot in the back.
"Accident-prone," said the family.

You always were cutting your hands
on rusty cans, running blindly
through broken glass, coming in
to the house lost about how

to explain to our wondering
mother what had happened
when you weren't even looking.
The world resisted quick explaining.

III.

In a few sessions of speech therapy,
holding on to sticks from which
paper fish dangled delicately,
you and I were asked to speak,

a stranger listening to our f's,
our faltering. Our tongues
still trip up the same way,
not a lisp or stutter exactly,

but our minds tumbling words
before we freeze into staring
at someone we've failed to reach.
We embarrass too easily.

I know for you I was embarrassing:
you pushed me down when I shouted

my happiness at your homecoming
in front of your friends.

IV.

At fifteen, I tried sleeping
with some of them, French-kissing
in front of you, until, one by one,
you gave the boys a talking-to.

When the police caught me and Vicky
spray-painting graffiti ("Peace,"
"Love," "Debbie B. fucks anything"),
you pleaded with Mom to punish me,

to take me in hand, watch over me.
You'd need to spend a few years
in tyrannical spirituality, living
in a shack, Volkswagen bus, a teepee,

until you discovered how easily
you could be accompanied, for you
were a beauty: men looked at you
when we cruised the avenue.

V.

You've thickened with responsibilities.
First wife, second wife, baby.
And I think you are always yelling.
I think you can't help being mean.

Words come out ugly, and the women weep,
then the women leave, and you don't
want any of this to be happening.
You mean to be gentle, to take care

of things, your days spent in Trauma,
directing emergencies, the aftermath
of individual catastrophes, the crashes
that take away our loves, our lives

(drunk on the highway, at home with knives),
calling me long distance late at night
where I reside on the other side
of the country, far from our family.

VI.

Last week, another of your stories:
taking your wife and baby down
the mountain for dinner and a movie,
trying to relax and take it easy

("let's try and take it easy"), you hit
what had just become an accident scene,
someone else's tragedy, a guy wiped out
on a bike (drinking), and you placed

your mouth on his mouth, his mouth filling
with his blood, and your mouth filling
with his blood, and you worked on him
until you were sick with it,

on your knees at the side
of the highway with dry heaves.
And you didn't save him.
Saving men isn't easy.

Girlfriends

We howled out our catcalls
to girls on the street from the safety
of her parents' four-door, blasting

rock 'n roll, reeking of Jean Naté,
watching their looks of pleasure
turn to surprise and dismay.

We always understood, we were only
stand-ins, props, doubles of each other,
the same smokes, combs, rings, eyes,

the other a part of our disguise
as we stood side by side,
waiting for guys to find us

barefoot in satin and taffeta,
abandoned ball gowns,
thirties negligées,

puka shells and sand dollars
in homemade macramé chokers,
moons and stars by our eyes,

bells in our ears, on our wrists, our feet,
everything jangling and calling out
all night with that pulse, that beat,

while by day we baked our bodies,
straightening our suits for clear lines,
coated in cocoa butter, Baby Oil, always

sweet and greasy, taking it easy, until
Jenny's breasts grew hard and heavy.
She had a hard abortion, not too early,

and we drank tumblers of gin, laughing
as we fell, and we took pills at Winchell's,
after eating half a dozen donuts each,

and we couldn't tell if we were
walking any longer or swimming
in the hazy light of a suburban street.

We spooned in mounds of fried rice,
downed cup after cup of sugared tea
in the broken-down mall they've torn down

to build something less beat, and we
made tuna tacos, double fudge brownies,
lemon meringue pies, quesadillas,

everything always greasy or sweet.
Tilting each other's heads to the light,
we applied white streaks of bleach

to the strands of our long, blond hair,
stood burned in backless sundresses,
beside the green ocean, waiting for men,

and we fell all over each other laughing
when they came, when they didn't come,
we fell all over, and Jenny had a baby

before we left each other's lives, she
to be the mother of four boys, the wife
of a drunk trucker into Harleys.

The last time we sat in the back seat
of her father's Impala, she asked me,
did I know what it tasted like, no,

so she pressed her breast, cupped
her hand for me and let me drink
the milk that had come from her body.

Sweets to the Sweet

It was another dead-end job,
and all things good in this world,
with its sweetness and light,

clean glass cases and flat stacks
of pleasing pink boxes
(admittedly a difficulty

to tie gracefully,
but what pleasant work
to pull down string

from several points in the air
and whip it around
rectangles and squares).

Pumpkin pies piled to the ceiling,
deep-dish, Dutch apple, mincemeat:
I mean, we made everyone happy.

Holidays, birthdays, anniversaries.
Or if they just wanted to stop in
for a little sweet at three.

Wedding cakes were a bustle for us,
finding the pillars and packaging,
as our beloved but distant decorator,

Sally Arrowhead, self-named,
having rejected patriarchy
after leaving her husband

and her husband's bakery,
complacently squeezed
out roses and leaves.

Though mostly it was slow,
often boring. There was nothing
much to say about anything.

The other full-time girl
was forty and interesting
just because she was

getting shots of baby urine
or placenta or something
to somehow stop her from eating.

Half her age, I too bloomed
below the waist, my hips
rounding out my dirty uniform,

the smuggled bits of old croissant,
squared-off brownies, slowly
reappearing in the curves of my body.

Of course, I was lonely, knowing
no one, seemingly invisible
in other shops, ignored on the street

except for the lunatics and beggars
who accosted me. One offered me
a torn rose, which I thought to take

until he gripped my hand in his
and dripped his blood on me.
He'd fallen, I guess, or been fighting.

Two weeks earlier was my first time
to see someone, a young woman,
get punched in the face.

She had tired of being tormented
by these boys on the bus, and she
had decided to say something.

But I don't think I was thinking of her
or thinking much of anything
as I waited to ride the 52

through the chill of North Berkeley
in early October, a dried-out coconut cake
boxed in my lap (too old to be sold

so I was pleased to take it home for free
despite its frosted football scene,
"One for the Gipper" iced in green).

A madman came and claimed
I was an angel, raving happily
at me until wandering away,

leaving me to lift the wallet
he'd left on the bench and palm
the folded bills, feeling awfully alone,

knowing I'd eat the aging cake and sleep
divided only by a flowered curtain
from my mother's life, until I woke

to work again, selling gingerbread men,
Mexican wedding cookies, and waiting
for something to happen to me.

Young Man at the Family Planning Clinic

The TV isn't working. And he isn't working.
He will lose a day's pay, and he's already
hurting. Having given the ledger lady

two hundred in twenties, he has only
a thin receipt left in the wallet of his jeans.
But it's lousy he should think such things.

Money shouldn't matter at times like these.
For her, it's a real tough day,
and he has only a small part to play:

to take her, and to pay, and to wait.
So he's waiting as discreetly as a young man
can be waiting for a young woman

at a place for family planning,
meaning women's problems:
birth control and pregnancy.

He combs his hair occasionally,
is careful not to jangle his car keys,
and he feels a little sleepy

from attempting to keep his face empty
all morning, to seem as if he could be
waiting for a second cup of coffee,

not wanting to be caught watching
any of the others as they move
through the swinging green doors,

or when they come out again, cotton
taped in the crooks of their arms,
to sit and flip through magazines

until those older women,
with soft hips and pink cheeks,
fling open a door with one hand,

the other holding folders, and call out
their names—"Maria, Theresa, Cathleen"—
to sweep them again into the inner sanctum,

into whatever rooms there are which he
will never see: the physicians, the machines.
For him, it's just bright walls, orange and pink,

Women's Day and *Good Housekeeping.*
Okay, but he's done all he can: he has
taken her, and he has paid, and he is waiting

until the moment when she's the one
who pushes through those doors alone.
Rising and putting her arm through his,

he is careful of her, not even looking
at her face, for her sake, just in case,
holding open the glass door to the street,

closing her slowly in his Chevy, letting
himself in on the other side, then letting
the engine idle while she leans her head

in the crook of his arm, and he wonders
at her warm body, the soft pink sweater.
She looks the same: clean and sweet.

Yet her breath seems to keep catching
on his sleeve, and he wants to say
something, maybe "I bet it wasn't easy."

But it's all her mystery,
and it will be her history to carry
past their breakup, which is impending,

so he pats her hair, her arm, her knee,
feeling like a witness at an accident scene,
that soon someone in authority will begin

to make inquiries (his name, his number,
who first entered the intersection
and if the light was green)

and that he is ready to answer
everything to the best of his ability,
knowing no one will ask

how he's feeling as they take away
the injured covered with sheets
and tow the wrecks to clear the streets.

Blackberry

I. I COULDN'T EAT

eggs, any way, mixed into solid yellow lumps,
or eye-open, wobbling. I kept thinking
of their delicate shells, the white holding

white, holding a yellow ball, holding.
Pushing them away, I poured myself
more milk, for it was cream to me

though nothing would grow from my own
womb's fruit, a blackberry briefly clinging
to this body. Everything else, vomited.

II. HIPS

Hers were just right to hook a child's leg
around. A young woman, she made her arms
into a cradle for my back, shifting the weight

away from her heart. Now fully grown, I am
all bone, in fashionable lines, breast to knee,
but sometimes when I drive alone in the hills

of Laguna, on curves smooth with fog, I think
of blackberries, my mother's summer dresses,
some roundness that's lacking in me.

III. SMALL BODIES

I keep dreaming of kittens who seem
to be dying because of me (if only I'd been
watching more closely), or they're simply

victims of a cruel world, or it's just
a crafty interplay between my failings
and their destiny. After whatever

catastrophe, I do what I can: rushing
through busy streets, pressing together
nasty gashes in their fur, making sure

their heads aren't on backwards,
pulling small bodies out of black water,
eye-dropping milk into tiny, dying mouths.

Sometimes they revive. More often,
I'm too late, inadequate, at fault, guilty.
And I wake to cradle nothing.

IV. CHAPEL OF FORGIVENESS

In San Francisco, my mother often goes
to Chinatown for tea or ginseng,
silk change purses, black canvas shoes.

She stops in to pray at Old St. Mary's
if she's weary, so it wasn't surprising
she proposed doing so with me.

After our stacks of saucers had been
assessed by the waitress, and we'd paid
for our Dim Sum, the little bits of heart

we ate in the shape of shrimps
rolled in white rice dough, slippery
pork bows, sweet black seed cakes,

we ascended the steps, feeling our way
in the dark entry to those dual chapels:
"Of Forgiveness," "Of Repentance."

She dipped her fingers in holy water
and sighed how she likes to choose
"Forgiveness" for everybody.

I said, "Hold on. Aren't you the one
who's supposed to need forgiving?"
I laughed until she laughed, and we collapsed

on the cement steps, tossing leftover pieces
of Chinese dumpling to the city pigeons as
they descended like a blessing upon us.

V. LIKE NEW

My skin is still young, like new silk
under my own tired hands in my own
bed alone. My poor feet are so cold,

the soles lonely, my eyes wide open,
but my heart rests inside this embrace
of ribs and beats out the years of life

left to me, my mother's, mine, and my
new dream of the blackberry, one
whose heart may beat beyond mine.

Panda Problems

I.

Meanwhile, it's spring. This is something
to be admitted freely. The zoo is free, and I am free
to go until summer hammers down the city, and we
are left inside to freeze. So I go, and I feel
how full of hope everyone is, waiting
for strange noises and joy in the panda pair.
Excited zookeepers look for signs: any unusual
chattering, walking backwards, that dance into mating.
Everyone hopes. Everyone knows they must hurry:
delicate, this breeding in captivity. A gift horse,
white elephant, these presents from China!
Happily, there's no doubt of their affection;
even with all of us watching, they chase each other
up imported trees, two mates wrestling,
though never for even as long as an hour:
these are zoo rules. Perhaps they need a break
from the constant mirror of black and white,
panda husband, panda wife.
A gentle resting: picking apart
blue leaves and drinking clean water,
the panda in isolation. A space from panda love.
But what happens if they stay together too long?
Is every panda an island? A philosophy?

II.

All day long scenes of the baby struggling
are replayed on TV. It doesn't look like anything
that could bloom into full panda splendor.
The proportions are all wrong, and it seems a joke
of nature, like the joey that worms its way
to the milky pouch of the mother kangaroo.
After tearful zoo people remove the dead offspring,
they tell the world they will watch for signs
of grieving, but they cannot measure what they see.
If there is a loss, it's a blank, a black and white mystery.

Looking into a Still Pool

A woman, bending
to retrieve the hem
of a blue
dress from the branch
that caught her stride.

*The water lilies
surrender.*

Lilies on the water.

Baptism.

A child's birth
into faith
at his mother's hand,
passing him to the Father,
to water.

*Branch loving
a woman's dress.*

A blue dress
drying on branches.
Someone has slipped
away to water.

Birth:

A child is pushed out
of water into water,
and the first thought
is regret.

A woman.

Birth.

Water.

A woman,
crouched by water,
is mending the tear
in her skirt.

Her cool body.

A pool of water.

Lilies.

A Small Cross

I. IN BERKELEY

Gentile:
heathen.
From late Latin, pagan.
Among Mormons, one who is not Mormon.

Shiksa.
Legs that are longer than his
though he strokes the gold down
of my thighs, on my carpet, in the sunlight.
Lovely, how lying together evens us out.

Christian
as distinguished from a Jew:
he kisses my neck above the small cross,
a remnant, hung from my throat. He closes
his eyes, presses my mouth shut,
and tastes my traditions
without meaning to.

II. IN BROOKLYN

As I spend my evenings smiling sadly,
he compares me with Modigliani's ladies,
long-necked and melancholy, making me
believe I have never been more beautiful
though I'm taller than all of his family,

and everything I do is wrong.
His mother is dying, and here I am,
mixing milk and meat, telling old refugees
how I loved Germany, whispering "Jesus,"
until he clamps his hand on my mouth

and begs for my silence in the bedroom
of his childhood, filled with Laurel and Hardy,
Simon and Garfunkel, dated girly magazines
(flips and false eyelashes) as I gladly
spend my nights in a boy's wet dream.

III. DEEPER IN BROOKLYN

I am at a loss, not softened by my hands
when I turn him to me, reaching in to new grief,
trying to retrieve a memory untouched
by the sanctity disappearing brings.

I'm at a loss when he cries into my breasts
until he recalls himself and kisses my lips, lost
when I listen to the rabbi's blessing: "A mother
of men, may the milk of her love be infinite."

The family sits shiva, and rounds of old people
funnel through the living room with its tasseled lamps,
enamels of pastel parakeets. Aunt Sylvia finds me
unveiling a mirror to paint my lips "Coral Reef."

I wrap up half-eaten food, clean invisible stains
on the drain board, until I can reasonably plead
backache and ascend to his boyhood bed
as Aunt Sylvia cries, "Where is she gone again?"

In the old row house, I falter when I'm not fucking him.
I pull our unwashed sheet over my head, tuck my hand
between my legs, swearing to remember that one woman
can't replace another and that I won't try.

IV. UPSTATE NEW YORK

As soft as snow is the low sound
of breathing as dreams of his mother
slide into the tips of his fingers.

In a shudder of memory, he reaches
for me, wanting the same dream,
complete understanding,

but on my side of the bed, I can feel
only a soft sorrow until I too fall
asleep, dreaming of blizzards,

of sounds drowning out,
the three of us all in white,
becoming clumps of separate ice.

Waking in sympathy,
I take him from one state
of sorrow to another.

When the Train

When the train moves, I'm not breathing
in right. Something's wrong, I know.
I try to make my heart slow down,
but in the backwards view of stray leaves,
trash on the tracks, I lose count, breathe fast,
and I know I'm going to fall.

I stopped inspiring, so you're breathing
the perfume of women, in bars, who know
you try, drinking so your mind slows down,
and some last hope of love and me leaves
you alone at last; I lose count, breathe fast,
and I know I'm going to fall.

The train moves, and my reason leaves me.
God! Who would catch me? Where are you?
No one will offer to let me sit down,
so I stand, swaying, my thoughts straying
to a stranger's sighs, which I count,
breathing fast, not falling.

When I moved, I thought you'd leave me,
for I thought I'd finally left you
after our lasting love had come down
to my rage and your straying
towards strangers, whom I count,
breathing fast, not falling.

When the train moves, I'm not breathing.
When I moved, I thought you'd leave me.
God, I knew I'd left you, I knew.
When I moved, love, I thought.
When the train moves, I'm not.

Mysterious Weather

It happens when you move. When you kiss
goodbye what you called home, you lose
even more than bargained for:
the sanity of understandable clouds.

In southern California, it was easy
to conquer the lines of earthquakes
in the cement of our sidewalks:
a game of cracks, a thrill.

The gentle rocking of the earth
was only a swollen promise of the future
fall of Babylon, for in the moment
of that past, all was lost

in a dreamy heat as Santa Anas blew
to a wild beat. You knew the signs:
your cat shooting straight up trees,
a sudden stillness, then the wind.

And because you grew on air,
on heat, you evolved a salty skin
and simple tastes for artichokes,
avocados, even the sea.

II.

Then you move. For reasons. You move,
and the sky opens up to mystery.
You go to New York and nearly choke
on the cold, coming to believe

you will freeze to death, your chilled
bones will break, kisses will always be
more pain than pleasure, and you believe
this has something to do with the weather.

It's easier to believe in your past,
so you learn to compare the snow:
pretty as the chemical flocking
on California Christmas trees.

Trudging in boots is like walking
barefoot across sand, but your green
ocean is a memory, and you find
you are left without any sort of plan.

III.

You didn't know moving keeps moving.
You didn't know you would move once
again until you'd retaped ten boxes
of the only home you have.

You didn't believe you really could be
heading to Texas until you hit Arkansas.
You never knew you'd live here
where the insects sound like snakes.

Not you, with your inappropriate sleeves,
pale knees. But you do, you are, and each
hour you seem to be less flesh, more water,
here where the days turn black with rain.

You find yourself living
where the land is sky,
not the earth rolling over,
but the sky breaking from the sky,

so you drive into a weather,
and all that you know of the world
dissolves into useless memories
of how that was and how this should be

as new weather denies
the religion of your past
and curls about your life
mysteriously.

Lessons in Space

Once again, a bad year for the skies.
Ice on the wings. Terrorist activities.

The shuttle shooting stars, a white blossoming,
newscasters suddenly speaking of the face of God

in the face of such large and instant beauty,
saying, surely that medley of men and women

has vaporized into angels. But on the beach,
a burned helmet, bone sliver from a slender foot.

Back in Houston, people explain things.
Just miscalculation, not God calling them up

with powerful love. But an error.
Technical. Human. Sufficient.

And I'm tanked on coffee, in a restaurant talking
to yet another friend who is losing

his mother; we're in our thirties.
Our parents have taken up dying.

But always the new wonder: my god, *my mother.*
Surgeons remove one piece at a time if they can;

still, the pain grows, and our mothers fade
into the pain before going away, for good,

forever, transformed into granite or ashes,
the smallest bone left on the beach,

the rest a miracle of disappearance
until pieces of bodies found in the water

are embedded instead in the earth, under stones
and flags. I'm afraid. The magic is failing.

When mothers can die, anything is possible:
the world is free to explode in white clouds.

And what do we learn but to loosen our fingers?
A shock that the living heart survives.

Cajun Wings and Loaded Skins

Tornadoes recently tore up Sweetwater, but those
who hid in their bathtubs had the wind
take only their roofs, not their lives, away.

One unhappy lady, down on her luck, dropped
all five of her brood, one by one, into the bayou,
but plans, like her mind, went awry, and not all died.

Cannibal mosquitoes. Killer bees. Coca-Cola on ice
in bed for me: summer in Houston is shocking. It heats up,
and old lovers shoot each other dead in their socks.

One man soaked his wife in gasoline, standing over her
with matches as she was sleeping in her dreams,
having come to understand the chances of her leaving.

I throw out old newspapers and end up alone
on a bus to San Antone, where I can see a monument
to our defeat, something smaller than it should be.

The boy selling ices across from the Alamo shades his eyes
and says he can tell where I'm from by my clothes,
but I don't know how, and I don't want to know.

All the way back, a young mother slaps at her baby,
but I meet a beautiful girl in blue jeans who smiles
and takes me to an ice house where I can buy her

Cajun wings and loaded skins, and she can explain
all about Frank, her sailor fiancé. I listen, for her eyes
are dusted pale blue all the way around, like clouds.

Frank's been stepping out with this brunette she says
"looks like she was rode hard and put away wet." Does this
make her more or less a threat? I still don't know

by the time I go to San Francisco for a holiday.
In a wine bar overlooking the bay, everybody laughs
when I do Texan accents. An art dealer explains,

"Texans buy the Impressionists for the bright colors."
I smile, but a picture postcard is in my pocket:
in a looping hand, circles over i's, the beautiful girl says,

"Hi. How's Frisco? Isn't it cold? Frank's leaving.
It's hot, the cicadas are crazy, but everything's blooming.
Come back, and we can follow the azalea trail."

A Train Is Going to Germany

A devil of a headache is in the making. I haven't been the same
since those three days drinking ouzo in a dive by the Acropolis,

dazzled by the clear stuff turning milky, imagining the twenties
and absinthe but sleeping only with invisible bed lice and you.

A French girl pulls down her jeans though everyone's looking.
A moment: legs and underpants. As she zips her shorts, she mocks

the pout of a small local boy though their bangs are the same.
There are also Swedes with little clothing but whiter teeth.

You and I are trying to leave Italy. We have no language
but our own to speak, so we travel slowly and stupidly.

In the station café, saucers and glasses scatter as a woman
slams her hand in a man's face, but nothing seems to break.

She kisses her insulted girlfriend, and they stay cheek to cheek.
I can't understand what I see, but I have a topless tan from Nice.

I'm not yet pregnant. You have trouble sleeping with me.
Slides will later show me as thin, brown, and dreamy.

In London, you'll start yelling. Though you'll threaten, you won't
    leave me
to get home on my own, not so long as we're out of the country.

You say, "A train is going to Germany." When I lean on you heavily,
you say, "Everyone's looking." On board, we'll sit by a man with chickens

and watch as he spoons himself milky stuff, mostly spilling. He'll point
to his stomach apologetically, and begin watching you and me.

He'll say he knows we're not married: we must be brother and sister!
Then he'll tell us we will need to leave these seats eventually,

for though we've paid, we have no reservations, and apparently
his family will soon be descending. "What do we do?" I say.

The man's wife will explain, waving her scarf out the window
as she stands in the aisle, a silent actress taking the breeze,

so we'll stand separately before sinking to the metal floor
near the roaring, wet restroom, where I'll cry until I start dreaming

though you won't be able to be rocked to sleep, and you won't
yet know you have tired of me, and I won't believe it.

A Blue Cup, with a Crack

I'm drinking green tea from a blue cup
with a crack down the middle. Where am I?

Morocco. And we're not leaving yet? No,
only moving to a hotel with less fleas.

Or so we believe. We believe everything.
And take none of it seriously.

How can we? We are the farthest
from home we'll ever be.

Camels move through the heat, cafés
fill with men, women's faces are shaded.

I've twisted my hair into a black scarf,
and I'm eating orange slices with sugar.

(The waiter keeps bringing them to me.
I can see we're not communicating.

When he nods at me so gaily,
I should not respond by smiling.)

Then it comes to me as I drink my tea:
I'm neither north nor south of it.

The oranges are bright orange, my cup
is blue, with a crack, here I am,

drinking tea and looking at my fingers,
at the center of the universe.

Univesity of Central Florida

Contemporary Poetry Series

Diane Averill, *Branches Doubled Over with Fruit*
George Bogin, *In a Surf of Strangers*
Van K. Brock, *The Hard Essential Landscape*
Jean Burden, *Taking Light from Each Other*
Lynn Butler, *Planting the Voice*
Cathleen Calbert, *Lessons in Space*
Daryl Ngee Chinn, *Soft Parts of the Back*
Robert Cooperman, *In the Household of Percy Bysshe Shelley*
Rebecca McClanahan Devet, *Mother Tongue*
Rebecca McClanahan Devet, *Mrs. Houdini*
Gerald Duff, *Calling Collect*
Malcolm Glass, *Bone Love*
Barbara L. Greenberg, *The Never-Not Sonnets*
Susan Hartman, *Dumb Show*
Lola Haskins, *Forty-four Ambitions for the Piano*
Lola Haskins, *Planting the Children*
William Hathaway, *Churlsgrace*
William Hathaway, *Looking into the Heart of Light*
Michael Hettich, *A Small Boat*
Ted Hirschfield, *Middle Mississippians*
Roald Hoffmann, *Gaps and Verges*
Roald Hoffmann, *The Metamict State*
Greg Johnson, *Aid and Comfort*
Markham Johnson, *Collecting the Light*
Hannah Kahn, *Time, Wait*
Michael McFee, *Plain Air*

Richard Michelson, *Tap Dancing for the Relatives*
Judith Minty, *Dancing the Fault*
David Posner, *The Sandpipers*
Nicholas Rinaldi, *We Have Lost Our Fathers*
CarolAnn Russell, *The Red Envelope*
Robert Siegel, *In a Pig's Eye*
Edmund Skellings, *Face Value*
Edmund Skellings, *Heart Attacks*
Floyd Skloot, *Music Appreciation*
Ron Smith, *Running Again in Hollywood Cemetery*
Katherine Soniat, *Cracking Eggs*
Don Stap, *Letter at the End of Winter*
Rawdon Tomlinson, *Deep Red*
Irene Willis, *They Tell Me You Danced*
John Woods, *Black Marigolds*